CONTENTS

Words in **bold** are in the glossary.

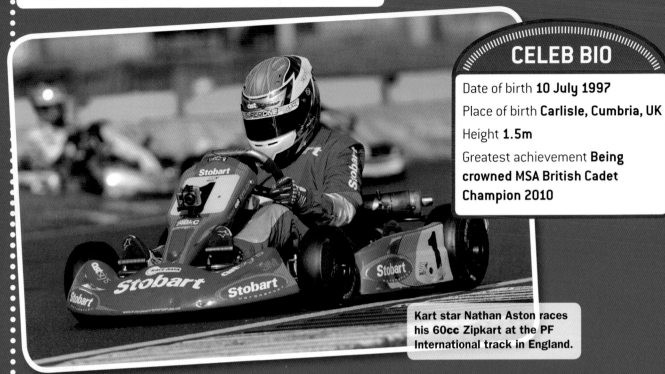

Kart star Nathan Aston races his **60cc** Zipkart at the PF International track in England.

NATHAN ASTON

Karting provides a competitive arena for young driving talents. The recently launched international Formula Kart Stars (FKS) series thrusts young racing hopefuls into the spotlight and offers them a path into Formula 1 (F1). FKS is heavily supported by F1 management and teams, who offer support and guidance to the competitors.

KART START

Many of today's motorsports stars began their careers in karting. Nathan Aston is one of the brightest karting stars around. Despite his age, he's already taken several titles and has been tipped to one day become an F1 driver!

RISING STAR

Aston's father took him for a fun day of karting when he was ten years old, and Aston fell in love with the sport. His natural talent was obvious and six months later he was signed to karting team Tooley Motorsport. In 2008 he won six **novice** races, and in 2009 he took part in his first FKS series. This was seen as a chance for Aston to learn the different tracks and to pick up as much as he could about kart racing.

BRITISH CHAMP

Aston performed well in the 2009 season, but the following season he **surpassed** everyone's expectations. In October 2010, 13-year-old Aston was crowned MSA British Cadet Champion in the FKS series (a title taken by Lewis Hamilton in 1996). His most impressive race was in Belgium where he beat all of his opponents by over 10 seconds – a gap virtually unheard of in the sport's highly competitive races.

CELEB ☆

MOTORSPORTS STARS

LAURA DURMAN

W

FRANKLIN WATTS

First published in 2011 by
Franklin Watts
338 Euston Road
London NW1 3BH

Franklin Watts Australia
Level 17/207 Kent Street
Sydney NSW 2000

ISBN: 978 1 4451 0533 8

Dewey classification number: 796.7'0922

A CIP catalogue record for this book is available from the British Library.

Planning and production by Discovery Books Limited
Editor: Laura Durman
Designer: D.R. ink

Printed in China

Franklin Watts is a division of Hachette Children's Books, an Hachette UK company.
www.hachette.co.uk

Photo acknowledgements: Getty Images: pp. 8 (Mark Thompson), 9 (Mark Thompson),
12 (WireImage/Jon Furniss), 15 top (Jasper Juinen), 15 bottom (Clive Mason), 18 (Robert
Laberge), 21 (Sports Illustrated/Bill Frakes), 24 (Franco Origlia), 27 top (Mark Thompson);
Kartpix.net: pp. 6 and 7 (Chris Walker); Rex Features: pp. 11 (Chris Walker), 22; Shutterstock
Images: pp. 10 (Digitalsport-Photoagency), 13 (Digitalsport-Photoagency), 16 (Murat Besler),
17 (B Stefanov), 20 (Warren Price Photography), 23 (Gustavo Miguel Fernandes),
25 (AMA), 27 (Julie Lucht).

Cover photos: Getty Images: centre (Hoch Zwei); Shutterstock Images: bottom left
(B Stefanov), bottom right (Walter G Arce).

Note to parents and teachers:
Every effort has been made by
the Publishers to ensure that the
websites in this book are suitable
for children, that they are of the
highest educational value, and
that they contain no inappropriate
or offensive material. However,
because of the nature of the
Internet, it is impossible to
guarantee that the contents of
these sites will not be altered.
We strongly advise that Internet
access is supervised by
a responsible adult.

'I just enjoy karting. Winning matters but losing isn't the end of the world.'

Nathan Aston holds his trophy for winning the Formula Kart MSA British Cadet Championship, 2010.

MSA British Cadet Championship 2010 Winner Round 1 Rowrah

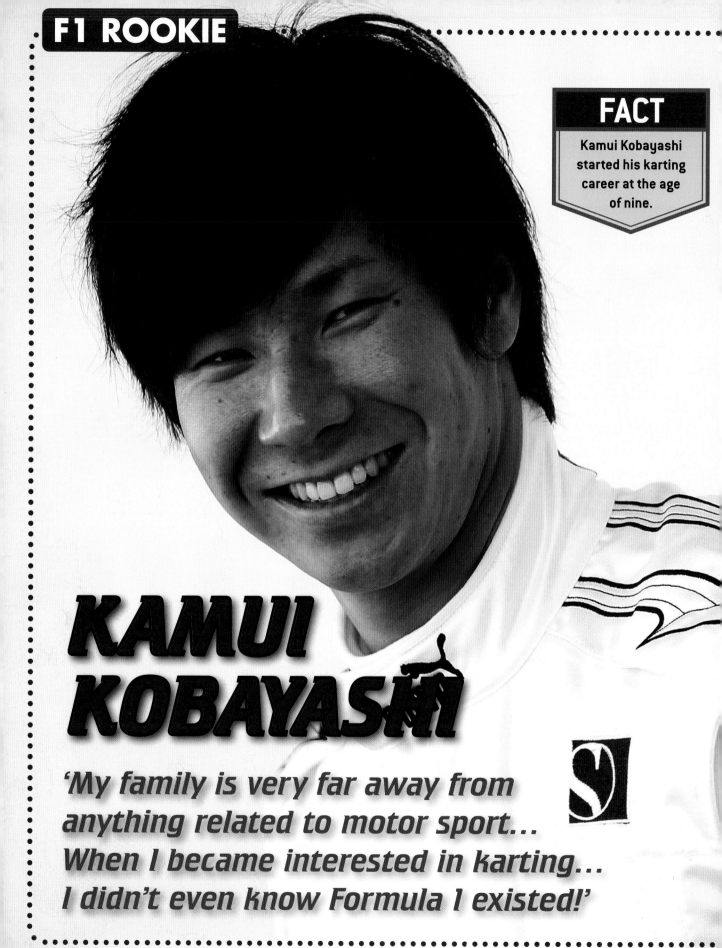

KAMUI KOBAYASHI

'My family is very far away from anything related to motor sport... When I became interested in karting... I didn't even know Formula 1 existed!'

The debut year of an F1 rookie's career is a testing time, and can decide their future in the sport. Rookies have generally risen up through the ranks of other motor sports and have already proven their skills and determination.

KARTING

Many talented young drivers, such as Japan's Kamui Kobayashi, start their careers on the karting track, racing in national and international competitions. Kobayashi won the All Japan Junior Kart Championship and the Suzuka Kart Championship aged 12.

TRAINING SCHOOLS

On the back of his karting success, Kobayashi was given a **scholarship** to the Esso Formula Toyota Racing School in 2001 aged 15. In 2004 he joined the Toyota Drivers Academy and competed in Formula Renault. The following year, at the age of 19, he won both the Formula Renault Eurocup and the Italian Formula Renault Championship.

FORMULA 3 AND GP2

Kobayashi was confirmed as a member of the Toyota Young Drivers Programme and stepped up into the world of Formula 3 in 2006. He was declared 'Rookie of the Year' and offered the chance to test an F1 car for the Toyota team. The next rung in the career ladder was a **stint** in the GP2 series. Although Kobayashi didn't dazzle in the main series, he won the 2009 GP2 Asia series with a 20-point lead.

F1 OPPORTUNITY

Kobayashi's F1 debut for Toyota finally came following Timo Glock's injury during the 2009 season. Kobayashi raced in his place in the Brazil and Abu Dhabi Grand Prix, catching the eye of several teams. With Toyota leaving F1, Kobayashi snapped up the offer from BMW Sauber-Ferrari to drive for them in the 2010 F1 season, and signed with them again for 2011.

Kobayashi takes part in the driver's parade at the Japanese Grand Prix, 2010. He finished the race in seventh place.

CELEB BIO

Date of birth **13 September 1986**

Place of birth **Hyogo, Japan**

Height **1.7m**

Greatest achievement **His outstanding performance in F1 during his rookie year**

K.Kobayashi

LEWIS HAMILTON

'To be racing in Formula 1 with McLaren has been the ultimate goal for me. It's a dream come true.'

Nine year-old Lewis Hamilton celebrates coming second in the Formula Cadet Championship.

Formula 1 rarely sees a talent like 2008 World Champion Lewis Hamilton. Lots of young karters dream of one day becoming an F1 World Champion. Not many are able to fulfil this dream!

KARTING PRODIGY

Lewis Hamilton has always had a passion for racing. At the age of ten he won his first British Karting Championship. That year, he famously approached the McLaren F1 team principal, Ron Dennis, and said 'I'm going to drive for you one day'. Three years later, Dennis signed him up to the McLaren driver development programme. Hamilton continued his karting career, and in 2000 he became the youngest ever karting world number one aged 15.

RACING CARS

Hamilton transferred his skills to car racing in the Formula Renault Winter Series 2001.

In 2003 he took the British Formula Renault title. He continued his impressive performance in the 2005 F3 Euro Series, winning 15 out of 20 races. Remarkably, he then took the championship title in his first GP2 season in 2006.

STEP UP TO F1

In 2007 Hamilton's dream came true when he joined the McLaren F1 team alongside double world champion Fernando Alonso. In his rookie year, Hamilton broke several world records and missed out on the championship by a single point. The following year he became F1's youngest ever champion (a record since beaten by Sebastien Vettel).

BOUNCING BACK

2009 was a disappointing year for Hamilton when the McLaren car failed to perform properly. A scandal then broke as it came to light that Hamilton had misled **race stewards** at the Australian GP in order to avoid a **penalty**. McLaren claimed that he had been told to do this by sporting director Dave Ryan, who was then fired from the team. However, the scandal soon died away, and Hamilton ended up finishing the season in top form with three **podium finishes** in the last four races. In 2010, he relished the challenge to work with (and beat) his new teammate – 2009 World Champion Jenson Button.

JENSON BUTTON

Formula 1 is one of the most exciting, competitive and glamorous motor sports in the world. Drivers enjoy international fame and multi-million-dollar salaries. They also get to drive extremely fast and unimaginably expensive cars for a living!

YOUNG PROMISE

Jenson Button excelled at karting, winning his first race aged eight in wet conditions from the back of the **grid**! He famously won all 34 races at the British Cadet Kart Championship in 1991. Having become the youngest winner of the European Super A Championship aged 17, it was obvious he was destined for great things.

PERFORMANCE AND PARTIES

Button's F1 debut came in 2000 when he was 20, making him the youngest British driver to start an F1 race. However his performance over the next few years was unremarkable, though some argued this was due to the cars he was given to drive. After 113 attempts, Button finally took his first Grand Prix win in Hungary in 2006. During this time Button had developed a **reputation** as a bit of a **playboy**. He made the most of the fame and attention that was thrust on him and was often seen at celebrity parties.

SUCCESS AT LAST

Button's **prospects** improved dramatically in 2009 when Brawn GP (formerly Honda) provided him with a car worthy of his talent. Button won six of the first seven Grand Prix, giving him an unbeatable lead. All his years of hard work finally paid off as he claimed the championship title. In 2010 he surprised many with his move to McLaren. His performances continued to impress, although he was not able to defend his championship title.

'I work really hard at Formula 1. It is therefore ok to do crazy things now and then.'

Button and his girlfriend, Jessica Michibata, arrive at the GQ Man of the Year awards in London. Although his playboy days may be behind him, Button still has a glamorous, celebrity lifestyle.

CELEB BIO

Date of birth **19 January 1980**

Place of birth **Frome, Somerset, UK**

Height **1.82m**

Greatest achievement **Winning the 2009 Formula One World Drivers' Championship**

RED BULL

Formula 1 is an intensely competitive sport. Drivers cannot achieve success on their own – they need a top team to back them up. British-based team Red Bull is proving itself to be one of the most successful teams, despite its relatively recent arrival in the sport.

SURPRISING INTRODUCTION

When F1 teams start out, they generally take time to settle into the sport. Red Bull launched an F1 team in 2005 and finished seventh out of ten teams in the final standings. This was an exceptional **feat** and an indicator of the success they would go on to achieve. In 2010, the Red Bull team took the **Constructors' Championship** with one race of the season still to go!

PRINCIPAL UNDER PRESSURE

Every F1 team has a team principal, such as Red Bull's Christian Horner. Horner is the man in charge on race day, and oversees decisions about everything from engineering to **strategy**. His ultimate aim is to do everything within his power to ensure that the drivers gain the most points possible in every race. He must also make sure that the drivers and team maintain a high position in both the Drivers' Championship and the Constructors' Championship.

DRIVER DRAMA

Top F1 drivers are extremely focused and competitive. Although F1 teams work together, driver **rivalry** can sometimes build if one is thought to be favoured over the other. For example, in July 2010 Red Bull developed a new front wing for their cars, but Sebastian Vettel's was damaged in practice. Horner made the controversial decision to take the new wing from teammate Mark Webber's car and put it on Vettel's. Many believed Horner favoured Vettel as the man most likely to win the Championship for Red Bull. Webber was said to be unhappy about the decision and, upon winning the race, joked 'Not bad for a number two driver!'

'Of course I want to beat [Mark] every time, and he wants to beat me, but we get along well.'

SEBASTIAN VETTEL

Christian Horner (below) celebrates at the 2010 Brazilian Grand Prix with race winner Sebastien Vettel (centre) and runner-up Mark Webber (left).

GRANDE PRÊ
PETROBRAS
BRA
SÃ PAULO 2

CELEB BIO

CHRISTIAN HORNER

Date of birth **16 November 1973**

Place of birth **Leamington Spa, Warwickshire, UK**

Greatest achievement **Becoming the youngest F1 Team Principal at the age of 32**

Check out the Red Bull team at www.redbullracing.com
www.sebastianvettel.com • www.markwebber.com

SEBASTIEN LOEB

Loeb races his way to win the WRC Rally of Turkey in 2010.

'...my motivation and my will to win are still as strong as ever!' LOEB, 2010

Sebastien Loeb is known as rallying's 'top dog' due to his astounding success in the sport.

The World Rally Championship is one of the toughest and most exciting motor sports in the world. Drivers face a series of two-, three- and four-day events in incredibly diverse **terrains** and driving conditions.

GREAT ADVENTURE

The WRC is sometimes described as the greatest motorsport adventure. It is certainly action-packed, with drivers, such as Sebastien Loeb, competing to perform under pressure and ultimately clock the best time. With races taking place against some of the most stunning landscapes in the world, the WRC provides a breathtaking spectacle for fans and spectators.

DOMINATING FORCE

Frenchman Sebastien Loeb grew up wanting to be a gymnast. However, as soon as he could afford his first car, he developed a love of driving and in 1995 he entered his first rally. Eight years later, Loeb created a stir in the World Rally Championship, challenging established drivers such as Colin McRae and Carlos Sainz, and becoming Vice-World Champion. The next year he won the championship, and the following year he became rallying's top dog when he broke all records with ten rally wins. Loeb now has six WRC titles to his name and continues to be a dominating force in the sport.

PERFECT PARTNERS

Every winning WRC driver has a talented and dedicated co-driver at his side. Loeb's co-driver, Daniel Elena, has been an essential part of his team for over ten years. Their partnership **flourished** during their first season together in 1998, and the pair have since celebrated many victories together. They are now considered one of the top crews in WRC.

CELEB BIO

Date of birth **26 February 1974**

Place of birth **Haguenau, Bas Rhin, France**

Height **1.71m**

Greatest achievement **Winning his first WRC championship 'because it was the achievement of a dream'**

DANICA PATRICK

Patrick poses at the Indianapolis Motor Speedway.

'The day before, the night before, the morning of, you can feel the weight and importance of the race. It's nerve-racking.'

Danica Patrick is undoubtedly the First Lady of US motor sport. With her glamorous looks, **forthright** manner and impressive driving skills, she is a force to be reckoned with both on and off the track!

THE EARLY YEARS

Patrick rose quickly through the ranks of the US karting circuit, winning several titles. Her passion and love for the sport was undeniable. As a determined 16-year-old, she dropped out of school and left home, moving to the UK to take advantage of the best training available to become a racing driver. Although she was too young to drive on British roads, she made her European debut in the Formula Vauxhall Winter Series in England in 1998.

A STEP UP

In 2000 Patrick entered the Formula Ford Festival at Brands Hatch, England, racing drivers including future F1 Champion Jenson Button. She achieved second place – the highest position gained by an American. She was already creating a major buzz in the UK and Europe, and in 2001 was awarded the Gorsline Scholarship Award for 'top upcoming road racing driver'. This was a **coup** for Patrick in the male-dominated sport, and attracted the attention of US racing team Team Rahal who quickly signed her up.

THE RACETRACK AND BEYOND

Patrick became the first woman to finish on the **podium** and to score a **pole position** in the North American racing series, the Atlantic Championship. In 2005 she entered her first **Indy 500** race, starting fourth and finishing fourth – the highest female starting and finishing positions in the history of the event. Since 2005 she has continued to break records and achieve success in the IndyCar Series, and has recently started to make a move into **NASCAR** racing. She has also become a major celebrity, appearing in adverts, music videos, magazines and on TV shows. She made her acting debut in a guest appearance on *CSI: New York* in 2010.

CELEB BIO

Date of birth **25 March 1982**
Place of birth **Beloit, Wisconsin, USA**
Height **1.57m**
Greatest achievement **Winning her first IndyCar race in 2008**

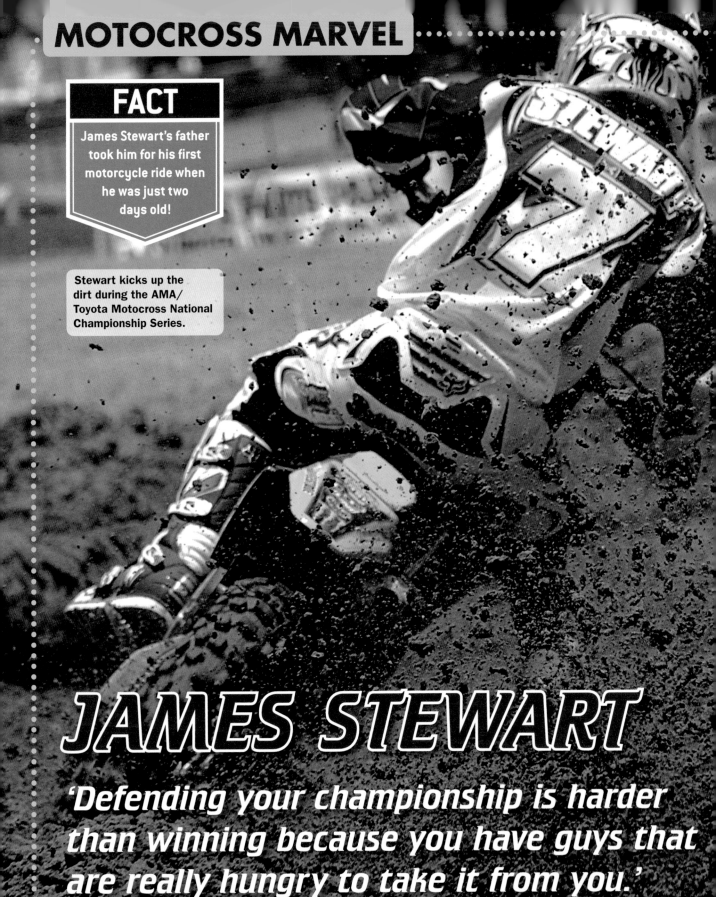

FACT

James Stewart's father took him for his first motorcycle ride when he was just two days old!

Stewart kicks up the dirt during the AMA/ Toyota Motocross National Championship Series.

JAMES STEWART

'Defending your championship is harder than winning because you have guys that are really hungry to take it from you.'

CELEB BIO

Date of birth **21 December 1985**

Place of birth **Bartow, Florida, USA**

Height **1.73m**

Greatest achievement **Being named 'Rookie of the year' in his debut pro season**

Stewart looking focused before going on to win the AMA Lites National Motocross Championship.

Motocross is a sport of guts, determination and raw skill. American racer James Stewart is one of its greatest talents and only the second rider in history to complete a perfect motocross season, 24 wins out of 24 races!

STARTING YOUNG

Amazingly, Stewart entered his first dirt bike race when he was just four years old! He went on to take the first of his 11 **amateur** titles at the age of six. He worked hard with his father to develop a unique riding style that constantly outperformed his competitors. During his amateur career he broke many records, including becoming the youngest rider ever to win the AMA Lites National Motocross Championship in 2002 when he was 16.

NO PAIN, NO GAIN

Stewart is an unpredictable and aggressive rider and has been plagued by injury throughout his professional career. What makes him exceptional is his ability to come back stronger after every injury. Returning from a broken collarbone, he won every race he entered in 2003. And it was after knee surgery that he went on to achieve his perfect motocross season in the 2008 AMA 125 Motocross National Championship. He suffered injury again in 2010, causing him to pull out of the 2010 AMA Pro Motocross series.

RAGING RIVALRY

The public rivalry between Stewart and fellow biker Chad Reed has been well documented. When Stewart dropped out of the 2008 Supercross Championship due to injury, Reed went on to take the title. The 2009 season proved interesting as Reed attempted to maintain his title, and Stewart fought to get it back. It was a close battle, but Stewart eventually took the Championship in the season finale in Las Vegas.

Check out James Stewart's website at js7.com

'To be a great motorbike racer, the most important thing is passion for the bike.'

VALENTINO ROSSI

Founded in 1949, MotoGP is the oldest motorcycle racing world championship. Today top motorcyclists, such as Valentino Rossi, compete in an increasingly fast and furious competition.

THE BASICS

There are three classes in MotoGP, and each class has its own race at every Grand Prix. The 125cc Championship features young riders who are taking their first steps into MotoGP. Moto2 (formerly 250cc class) is for more experienced riders and now features more powerful 600cc bikes. The MotoGP Championship (formerly 500cc class) tests the finest talents, using explosive 800cc bikes and reaching speeds of up to 349 kph (217 mph). Each championship requires different skills and the bikes **handle** differently. Winning in one of the lower categories does not guarantee success in the higher groups.

TOP TALENT

Valentino Rossi is one of the most gifted riders in the MotoGP Championship. His debut came in 1996 when he entered the 125cc class at the Malaysian Grand Prix. He finished the season in 9th position. The following year he became the youngest ever champion, aged 18. He became World Champion of the 250cc class in 1999 and the 500cc class in 2001. He then held onto the MotoGP World title from 2002 to 2005.

MR PERSONALITY

Rossi is known as one of the biggest personalities in the sport. He is famous for his jokes, pranks, wacky helmets and comedy victory celebrations (which he often thinks up in advance with the help of his fans). In 2007 ten of his friends dressed up as bowling pins and waited at the side of the track. Rossi celebrated his win by pretending to bowl them all down, achieving a strike.

CELEB BIO

Date of birth **16 February 1979**

Place of birth **Urbino, Italy**

Height **1.82m**

Greatest achievement **Aged 18 the youngest ever rider to win the 125cc World Championship**

Prankster Rossi usually sports a funky helmet of some sort. In 2008 he started a trend of wearing helmets personalised with your own face. He said that this picture shows his expression when he takes a corner at over 300 kph (186 mph)!

Rossi waves to the crowd at the Portuguese Grand Prix.

FACT

Rossi's father, Graziano, was also a great biker. Valentino was born in 1979, the year Graziano took his first 250cc GP win.

SUPERBIKE STAR

MAX BIAGGI

Italian Max Biaggi is one of the most popular motorcycle racers in the world today.

CELEB BIO

Date of birth **26 June 1971**

Place of birth **Rome, Italy**

Height **1.7m**

Greatest achievement **Winning the 2010 World Superbike Championship**

The World Superbike Championship (WSBK) is one of the most exciting motorcycle racing events. Unlike MotoGP, which features specially built bikes, WSBK riders race finely tuned versions of the bikes that we see on our roads. As in F1, teams compete for a manufacturers' championship as well as a riders' championship.

'...racing isn't just about speed, tyres and an engine. It is also about jc and having fun...'

RACING LINKS

The worlds of superbikes and MotoGP are closely linked. Most riders begin racing in WSBK and move on to MotoGP. However, some drivers switch between the two, and others move across from MotoGP to WSBK. One such driver is four-time World Champion Max Biaggi.

YOUNG BIAGGI

Max Biaggi pursued a football career until his friend took him to a motorcycle racetrack. This moment changed his life forever. He began his racing career at the age of 18. He won the 250cc World Championship four years in a row between 1994 and 1997. Biaggi then enjoyed successful years in the 500cc and MotoGP classes, though the championship title **eluded** him.

SUPERBIKE SWITCH

In 2007, following a year off from racing, Biaggi joined the Corona Alstare Suzuki team to race in WSBK. He won his first race and, after a hard season, finished third overall. In 2009 he signed with Aprilia (the company with whom he won the 250cc World Championships). Despite speculation that both Biaggi and Aprilia were past their peak, they went on to win both the Riders' World Championship and the Manufacturers' Championship in 2010.

FACT

Biaggi is the only rider to have won his very first race in both the 500cc Championship and World Superbike Championship.

DAVID COULTHARD

Only the best drivers in the world get to be an F1 driver, but their racing career cannot last forever. Drivers often stay involved in the sport in some way after they retire from racing. Well-respected F1 driver David Coulthard now appears as a TV **pundit** for the BBC, as well as working on other projects.

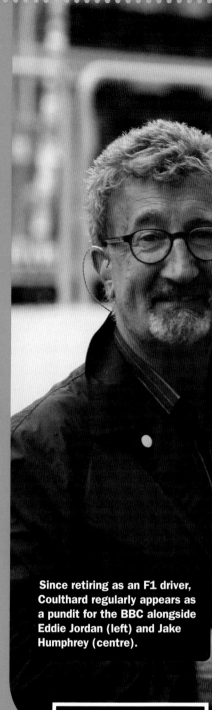

Since retiring as an F1 driver, Coulthard regularly appears as a pundit for the BBC alongside Eddie Jordan (left) and Jake Humphrey (centre).

EARLY CAREER

David Coulthard **test-drove** for the Williams team for a couple of years before becoming a full-time F1 driver in 1995, teaming up with F1 legend Damon Hill. That year he enjoyed his first win at the Portuguese Grand Prix and finished third in the F1 Championship. After he moved to McLaren in 1996, Coulthard really began to raise his profile in the sport. During the nine years Coulthard spent with them he notched up 12 of his 13 Grand Prix wins and had 51 podium finishes.

HIGH SCORES

In 2005 Coulthard became a driver for the newly formed Red Bull team. He relished the challenge of starting afresh and helping to develop the car with chief designer Adrian Newey. Coulthard consistently won points for the team, as well as many races. By the time Coulthard retired in 2008 he had collected 535 points, making him the highest scoring British F1 driver of all time.

THE NEXT PHASE

Following Coulthard's success as a Red Bull driver, the team invited him to continue work with them as a consultant. He focuses mainly on the testing and development of the team's cars. He writes F1 articles for the press and regularly appears as a pundit on the BBC's F1 coverage, as well as being offered the role of commentator in 2011. He also acts as an ambassador for Mercedes-Benz and has recently begun to race for them in the German Touring Masters (DTM).

FACT

At Williams, Coulthard replaced legendary driver Ayrton Senna after Senna's fatal accident during the 1994 San Marino GP.

'Life, if you're lucky, is long and you have different things in different phases, so I'm into another phase of my life now.'

CELEB BIO

Date of birth **27 March 1971**

Place of birth **Twynholm, Dumfries and Galloway, UK**

Height **1.82m**

Greatest achievement **Two home Grand Prix wins at Silverstone**

Coulthard getting ready to race for Red Bull at the British Grand Prix at Silverstone.

Check out David Coulthard's website at www.davidcoulthard.co.uk

amateur Somebody who takes part in a sport on an unpaid basis.

cc Cubic capacity. It is the measure of the engine size of a motorbike.

Constructors' Championship The championship in Formula 1 in which the most successful team is crowned champion. The points gained by both team drivers are added together in this championship.

coup A triumph, achievement or highly successful act.

Drivers' Championship The championship in Formula 1 in which a driver is named World Champion.

elude To fail to attain or achieve something.

feat A great achievement that requires skill, strength or courage.

flourished Developed quickly and successfully.

forthright Outspoken and direct.

grid The lines that mark the starting places on a motor racing track.

handle The way a vehicle functions while being driven.

Indy 500 The Indianapolis 500 (shortened to Indy 500) is a 500-mile race that takes place in the USA each year at the Indianapolis Motor Speedway in Speedway, Indiana.

IndyCar Series The top car racing Championship in the USA.

NASCAR The National Association for Stock Car Auto Racing.

novice Describes an event for inexperienced racers.

penalty A punishment.

playboy A young man who likes to party and live a celebrity lifestyle.

podium The winners' platform where the drivers or riders who came first, second and third in a race are given prizes.

podium finish Coming first, second or third in a race, and therefore taking a place on the winners' podium.

pole position First place on the grid.

prospects Chances of success.

pundit An expert who appears on television or in other media to express an opinion on something.

race stewards Race stewards make sure races are conducted properly and enforce the rules.

reputation The opinion that is held about somebody (rightly or wrongly).

rivalry Intense competition.

rookie A sportsperson in his or her first year.

scholarship If you have a scholarship, your studies are paid for by the school, university or an organisation.

stint A short amount of time.

strategy A plan of action that is designed to achieve success.

surpass To be greater than or exceed.

terrain Land.

test-drive To drive a vehicle in order to test its performance.

tuned Adjusted for maximum performance.

FURTHER INFORMATION

BOOKS

21st Century Lives: Motorsports Champions by Paul Mason (Wayland, 2007)

Go Turbo: Formula 1 by Tom Palmer (Franklin Watts 2010)

Graphic Careers: Racing Car Drivers (Franklin Watts, 2010)

Inside Sport: Motorsports by Clive Gifford (Wayland, 2009)

Motorsports: Formula 1 by Clive Gifford (Franklin Watts, 2009)

Motorsports: Karting by Clive Gifford (Franklin Watts, 2009)

Motorsports: Motorcycles by Clive Gifford (Franklin Watts, 2009)

Motormania: Racing Cars by Penny Worms (Franklin Watts, 2010)

WEBSITES

http://www.formula1.com
The official F1 website.

http://www.formulakartstars.com
The official Formula Kart Stars website.

http://www.motocross.com/moto
A website containing motocross news, features and race information.

http://www.motogp.com
The official website for the MotoGP championships.

http://www.worldsbk.com/en/home.html
The official World Suberbike Championship website.

http://www.wrc.com
The official World Rally Championship website.